Spirituality, Stress & You

Thomas E. Rodgerson

D0826683

Paulist Press
New York/Mahwah, New Jersey

Cover/book design and interior illustrations by Nicholas T. Markell.

Library of Congress Cataloging-in-Publication Data

Rodgerson, Thomas E., 1950-
    Spirituality, stress & you / Thomas E. Rodgerson.
        p.   cm. — (Illumination book)
    ISBN 0-8091-3514-0 (pbk.)
    1. Spiritual life—Christianity.   2. Stress—Religious aspects—
Christianity.   I. Title.   II. Title: Spirituality, stress, and you.   III.
Series: IlluminationBooks
BV450.1.2.R624   1994   94-31705
248.8'6—dc20   CIP

Published by Paulist Press
997 Macarthur Boulevard
Mahwah, New Jersey 07430

Printed and bound in the
United States of America

Contents

IlluminationBooks
A Foreword

*I*lluminationBooks *bring to light wonderful ideas, helpful information, and sound spirituality in concise, illustrative, readable, and eminently practical works on topics of current concern. Learning from stress; interior peace; personal prayer; biblical awareness; walking with others in darkness; appreciating the love already in our lives; spiritual discernment; uncovering helpful psychological antidotes for our tendency to worry too much at times; and important guides to improving interpersonal relations are only several of the areas which will be covered in this series.*

The goal of each IlluminationBook, then, is to provide great ideas, helpful steps, and needed inspiration in small volumes. Each book offers a new beginning for the reader to explore possibilities and embrace practicalities which can be employed in everyday life.

In today's busy and anxious world, Illumination-Books are meant to provide a source of support—without requiring an inordinate amount of time or prior preparation. Each small work stands on its own. Hopefully, the information provided not only will be nourishing in itself but also will encourage further exploration in the area.

. One is obviously never done learning. With every morsel of wisdom each of these books provides, the goal is to keep the process of seeking knowledge ongoing even during busy times when sitting down with a larger work is impossible or undesirable.

However, more than information (as valuable as it is), at the base of each work in the series is a deep sense of *hope* that is based on a belief in the beautiful statement made by Jesus to his disciples and in turn to us: "You are my friends" (Jn 15:15).

As "friends of God" we must seek the presence of the Lord in ourselves, in others, in silence and solitude, in nature, and in daily situations. IlluminationBooks are designed to provide implicit and explicit opportunities to appreciate this reality in new ways. So, it is in this Spirit that this book and the other ones in the series are offered to you.

—*Robert J. Wicks*
General Editor, IlluminationBooks

Chapter One
Introduction

"He leads me beside still waters; he restores my soul" *(Psalm 23:2).*

Stress may not be peculiar to our age, but it is certainly pervasive and persistent. Ours is an age of rapid social change, the result of increased population growth, technology and new knowledge. Ours is an age of institutional breakdown, whether in the area of banking, education, government or religion, which leaves us without a secure structure for our lives. Ours is an age of apparently unsolvable problems whether in the area of international politics or physical disease. Ours is an age of diminishing returns where we have to work harder just to stay even.

Whereas acute stress used to occur in our lives every ten years, it now occurs every two years. Such acute stress is not only the result of major life traumas but also the build-up of what researchers call "daily hassles." An uncooperative spouse, having to fight traffic, a co-worker's smoking, a noisy neighbor all contribute to the build-up of our stress.

Ours is also a health conscious age, and we have been made aware of the contribution of stress to our physical health. Excess stress has been associated with the following disorders: heart disease, high blood pressure, diabetes, headaches, obesity, ulcers, backaches, asthma, arthritis, depression, anxiety, alcoholism, insomnia, diarrhea, constipation, colitis, hay fever, sexual dysfunction, menstrual problems, and cancer. As well, Hans Selye has pointed out that stress contributes to aging. After a stressful period rest can restore us *almost* to the original level of fitness, but not quite. This difference adds up to what we call aging.

Just as we are not going to eliminate aging from life, neither will we eliminate stress. Stress is a part of life in every age. In every age sickness happens, death occurs, danger arises. In a time of far less population growth and change the writer of the Twenty-third Psalm obviously had known great stress in order to give such value to the restoration of the soul.

What might have been a source of stress for the writer of the Twenty-third Psalm might not be a source of stress for you or for me. And even in our own age the chaos of change creates stress for some and not for others. What some persons see as a threat others see as a challenge. Stress, then, has something to do not only with what is happening outside of us (an external stressor), but also with what is happening inside us (how we perceive the stressor).

From the start it is important for us to perceive stress as something that cannot and should not be eliminated from life. Our task is to manage stress and to learn from the stress of life.

Stress in biological terms is a state of readiness. When something is perceived as a stressor the brain sends alarm messages that prepare the body for fight or flight. If we were surprised by an intruder we might choose to fight or flee. But the body's reaction would be the same either way as muscles tighten, senses heighten, and heart and breathing rates increase. Such a state of readiness is to our advantage for survival. It only becomes a problem when we are in a state of readiness for prolonged periods of time due to constant stressors around us, or due to our peculiar perception of events around us that we interpret as threatening.

In spiritual terms we might think of stress as a call to wake up: to take a closer look at the way we are living our lives; to take a closer look at our inner selves; to take a closer look at our spiritual health. Perhaps in the stresses of life we are being called to wake up and take notice that we have wandered too far from the "still waters," or that we have refused the leading of God who would restore our soul. The twelfth-century mystic, Hildegard of Bingen, could speak of salvation as a "wetness" that brings powerful life to the soul and of the Holy Spirit as bringing a "merciful dew" into the human heart to overcome dryness.

In times of stress there is the very real danger that we will "dry up" and that physically, mentally and spiritually we will suffer. Acknowledging that we will never eliminate all the stress in our lives, our task becomes to maintain a vital "wetness" even when the heat is turned on.

Chapter Two
Stress and Our Bodies

"For my people have committed two evils: they have forsaken me the fountain of living waters, and hewed out cisterns for themselves, broken cisterns, that can hold no water"
(Jeremiah 2:13).

I remember a trip on a scorching June day along the western edge of the Dead Sea to the famous fortress of Masada. Masada was the scene of the last stand of Jewish rebels who began a revolt against the Romans in A.D. 66. It took the Roman army five years to overcome the rebels ensconced behind the walls of Masada because the impregnable fortress sits on the flat top of a mountain that has sheer rock faces rising 800 feet above the valleys below.

But how could anyone survive for five years atop a mountain where there are no streams, no springs, no wells, and where it does not rain at all for much of the year? The way they survived was by carving out huge cisterns in the rock and developing an intricate system for catching water during the rainy season. This water held in reserve would then carry them through the dry period of the year.

Reserves of energy

One way that we deal with stress is by maintaining a reserve of energy that can carry us through the difficult moments of life. That reserve of energy is actually stored in our bodies. Hans Selye referred to this energy as "adaptation energy" used by the body in adapting to stressors. He felt that each of us is given a limited amount of adaptation energy, and we must budget it accordingly. When we rest we can draw upon reserves of adaptation energy from various places in the body, but if there is a continuous drain, or a failure to restore this energy, eventually it is all used up. When the energy is used up exhaustion sets in, followed by disease in the weakest part of the body, and eventually followed by death.

Just as the Jewish rebels at Masada needed those reserves of water to survive a long-term siege, so we too need reserves of energy in our bodies to encounter the stresses of life. Yet many of us operate with "leaky cisterns" when it comes to our bodies, letting the vital energy of life stored in our bodies leak away unnecessarily.

Building reserves through diet

Poor diets and poor eating habits are like having leaky cisterns that drain away vital energy which is needed in stressful times. Certain chemical substances called sympathomimetics are contained in certain foods. These sympathomimetics actually trigger a stress response in the body. One sympathomimetic substance is caffeine that is found in coffee, tea, cocoa, chocolate, and many soft drinks. The amount of caffeine in one or two cups of coffee can actually trigger a stress response in the body.

Eating concentrated amounts of sugar also makes the body work harder. When blood sugar rises quickly the body overreacts with insulin and drives the sugar out of the blood into the cells. Then the normal blood sugar needed by the brain is reduced, and a person having initially felt a surge of energy will soon begin to feel tired and irritable. Eating the "famous" American breakfast of coffee and doughnuts is like going off to face the stress of the day with a leaking cistern that is draining away vital energy before we even start.

Besides reducing caffeine and sugar intake we might consider the following to help build the reserve of energy in our bodies:

1. Eat more fruits, vegetables, whole grains, legumes, nuts and seeds, preferably grown organically.

2. Replace processed foods with homemade or fresh foods.

3. Reduce salt intake.

4. Use less fatty meat such as bacon, ham, sausage, beef, and pork.

5. Limit the number of eggs eaten.

6. Eat breakfast each day and regular meals throughout the day.

7. Take a vitamin supplement with a strong B-complex in stressful times.

Building reserves through proper sleep

When we operate in stressful times without proper sleep it is like facing the dry seasons of life with a leaky cistern. In my first pastorate a wise woman in her nineties often confronted me after the morning worship service saying, "You are operating without any reserve of energy. I can see it in your eyes. Go home and take a nap before you wear your body out." Often I had been up late the night before trying to finish a sermon, and then I would rise early to prepare for a full day of services.

This perceptive woman was not only offering me some practical advice about how to prepare myself for the stress of ministry but also was confronting me with the spiritual issue behind my lack of sleep. It was the Psalmist who wrote, "Unless the Lord builds the house, those who build it labor in vain. Unless the Lord watches over the city, the watchman stays awake in vain. It is in vain that you rise up early and go late to rest, eating the bread of anxious toil; for he gives to his beloved sleep" (Ps. 127:1-2). Spiritual issues of trust and surrender surfaced from behind my tired eyes and lack of sleep.

There is, then, in our sleeping the practical and the physical. Our bodies need rest. We need a reserve of energy in stressful times that comes through a rested body. But even more, our sleeping reflects to some extent our way of living. While it is true that people will vary in the amount of sleep they need and while it is true that some persons have biological factors that affect their sleep, our style of sleeping tells us something about how we live our lives. Sleeping too little, or sleeping too much, sends us the message that we are choosing to live with leaky cisterns rather than with full cisterns.

Building reserves through exercise

Doctors have commented that the lack of physical exercise is the most serious health hazard facing us in this country. Vigorous exercise can suppress hunger, stimulate creativity, fight depression, reduce weight, and reduce stress. If we are not regularly exercising we are living with a leaky cistern that will soon run dry!

During my seminary days I had a mentor who was ninety-six years old. This deeply spiritual and very alive woman continued an active life of working until just two weeks before she died at the age of ninety-eight. She ate mostly fish, fresh fruits, and vegetables. She slept well at night—usually with the window open despite the Scottish gales! And she walked the Blackford Hills three times a week without fail.

Twenty minutes a day, three times a week is all it takes to build our physical reserves with exercise. Running, swimming, biking, or taking a brisk walk prepares the body for the stress of life. While we think that it does not hurt to let a week, or a month, or a year go by without exercise, what is happening is similar to a growing leak in our cistern. One day we will go to the cistern and it will be dry.

The apostle Paul could speak of the spiritual life as running a race and of pummeling his body and subduing it as preparation for that race (1 Cor. 9:24). Exercise is one way that we prepare our bodies and our selves for the race of life.

Building reserves through relaxation

Herbert Benson found in his research that by teaching people to relax, hypertension could be lowered or eliminated for many people. Learning a simple form of relaxation could alter the physiological stress on the body he discovered. Later he found that combining simple relaxation exercises with a person's deep spiritual beliefs enhanced the well-being of the person even more. Benson recommended that at a set time twice a day a person find a comfortable position, close their eyes, relax their muscles, become aware of their breathing and, with a passive attitude, focus on a phrase or word that is central to their belief system.

If we would simply include our bodies in our daily prayer time we could build a reserve in our bodies that would help us face the stress of life. By this I mean to take the time in our daily prayer time to give thanks for our body and then to take a few moments to let the body relax. Sometimes I like to think of the tension in each muscle rolling off and onto the floor. Sometimes I like to think of the light of Christ filling and warming each part of my body. Then, becoming aware of my breathing, I focus on an ancient prayer of the church—breathing in and saying, "Lord Jesus Christ," and breathing out saying, "have mercy on me."

Building reserves by valuing the body

It may seem peculiar to begin a book on spirituality and stress by talking so much about the body. Yet there is a very real physical component to stress. Stress wears on the body and attacks its weakest part. We cannot deal with stress without taking care of the body.

Yet there is a deeper issue that emerges here. Often in Western Christianity there has been a devaluing of the body. At best the body was something taken for granted. At worst the body was something that was evil. Either way we often split our spiritual selves from our physical selves. I would say that this sets up an inherent tension in our souls, a virtual tearing of ourselves in two. This in itself creates an inner stress for living.

Before we will ever attend to diet, or sleep, or exercise, or relaxation we will have to value the body. We will have to see the body as an important part of who we are and what we do. We will have to see the body as an important part of our spiritual journey given to us by the Creator.

The Christian faith is truly incarnational. God comes in human flesh. The meaning of life is found where flesh and spirit meet. Not valuing the flesh in appropriate ways robs life of meaning and sets up within us an inherent stress. It is like living with a leaky cistern.

Chapter Three
Stress and Our Environment

"God is our refuge and strength, a very present help in trouble. Therefore, we will not fear though the earth should change, though the mountains shake in the heart of the sea.... There is a river whose streams make glad the city of God, the holy habitation of the Most High. God is in the midst of her, she shall not be moved" (Psalm 46:1-5).

Each of us has a unique environment in which we live, and that unique environment has its own unique stressors. If we were lying on a beautiful beach where the sun is perfect and the water is perfect, for most of us the environment would be filled with very few stressors. If, however, we were living in the inner city in a row house with no screens on the windows, no air conditioning, the temperature at 102 degrees, constant noise outside the window, and crime in the streets, the environment would be very stressful for most of us. Other factors might influence our experience of stress in these situations, such as how we were to think of the above situations (e.g., perhaps I hate the sun or am afraid of the water), or how we got along with the people around us in those situations, but the environment itself could contribute to that stress.

Many factors contribute to our unique environment. In this chapter we will look at "daily hassles," time, and money as factors that contribute strongly to the atmosphere in which we live. With each of these there can be a reduction of stress when we become aware of the stress they cause and take corrective action: action grounded in our own life purpose and in a higher perspective on the events of life. It is as if our life needs a river to run through it. Like those who built ancient cities around the river, so our lives are built around a purpose, and the purpose is connected to something that comes before it and flows beyond it.

Dealing with daily hassles

Researchers have discovered that daily troublesome events can produce more stress in the life of a person than major life events. It is the little things that seem to matter, pushing us to our adaptive limits and to the edge of stress. Traffic jams, noise, pollution, cigarette smoke, lines, over-crowding, broken equipment, clutter, inadequate resources, tight schedules and deadlines, etc. are environmental factors that contribute to the daily stress in our lives.

Many of these factors we no longer notice, or give little attention. A first step in dealing with our daily hassles is to begin to notice them. We can take a note card around with us and begin to observe the little annoyances of life. Once we observe them we can make plans to do something about them. If the paint in the room is a depressing color then we can make plans to change the color. If the lighting bothers our eyes then we can work to change the lighting. If the traffic is a bother we need to think of alternative ways to get to work, or even begin to make long-term plans to move.

However, decisions about daily hassles need also to consider our purposes for life. Each year it is a wise idea to set out goals for our lives. What do we want to accomplish this year? How does it fit in with my career goals or goals for my family? What is the shape that I want my life to take? We can make yearly goals, five-year goals, or life-long goals.

Sometimes we will tolerate certain daily hassles because they fit in with our goals. A longer commute may be a hassle, but it makes possible an education or enables us to make a career move without an unnecessary disruption to family life. Usually such toleration is possible because we have a goal in mind with a time limit on how long we must cope with such a hassle.

Sometimes our decisions about daily hassles come into focus with our life purposes in mind. Perhaps the way the furniture is arranged is not meeting our needs. We need a central place to do our work in the house rather than the hassle of shifting from one table top to another. Or we need a place where we can relax and the kids can be kids without worrying about the mess.

Yet daily hassles also call us to a higher perspective. This holds true even when the hassles are beyond our ability to change. What is the daily hassle telling me about me? Why do I respond with fury to the traffic jam or to the boss at work? Is the problem event giving me clues about how I live my life? Are the hassles telling me that I need to look for purpose in my life? Are the hassles calling me to a higher source of help in God?

Certainly those who survive in an environment like the inner city with any degree of health must have a sense of purpose, even if that purpose is survival itself. And often there is held a higher image of what life is about and the support that comes from God.

Managing money

Dealing with money can be a daily hassle. Yet it so influences the atmosphere in which we live that it deserves to be discussed separately. While there may be some persons who are hassled by what to do with all their money, for most of us the hassle comes from never having enough money. Lack of financial resources, for whatever reason, puts a tremendous stress upon an individual or family. Sound financial planning, on the other hand, can provide a cushion to soften the blows that might come from stressors in other areas of our lives.

For example, when we are already stressed at work or with family pressures it seems never to fail that the car will break down, or an appliance in the home will stop working. If we have reserves from which to draw, the additional stress of such a breakdown will be far less than if we have to scrape the money together from somewhere and create a financial crisis on top of everything else. Or, as another example, if we have made a budget that includes setting aside money for vacations or entertainment, we have resources available to get away for a few days when stress begins to build in our lives.

Building a reserve fund that acts as a cushion, or simply preparing for upcoming major expenses such as an insurance policy or car maintenance, is easily accomplished through simple budgeting. Budgeting takes the chaos out of our spending and directs that spending to our desired purposes. The ability to save money actually is accomplished through the elimination of waste. Money that is not directed through a budget is usually "blown" and we have no idea where it has gone. Budgeting eliminates the waste by directing our spending.

Building a reserve also can come from becoming cautious about any debt. Many persons could create a healthy savings account with the money that they are now

spending to pay the interest on their credit cards. To have the money before we spend it is not only good financial advice but aids in the elimination of stress. Even in major purchases such as a house or a car we can reduce the interest paid and reduce the stress in our lives by not borrowing the maximum allowed. Instead of stretching ourselves to the limit of what we can afford, we can buy something more affordable and leave room for emergencies or savings.

Budgeting further reduces stress in our lives when it reflects our goals and life purposes. Even our spending of money can reinforce a sense of harmony and direction in our lives, like a river following a clear-cut channel. If we value education, our saving and spending needs to reflect that. If we value recreation, our saving and spending needs to reflect that. If we value serving others, if we value the work of the church, if we value justice, ecology, or evangelism, our saving and spending needs to reflect that. Stress is reduced by bringing our money matters into harmony with the purposes of our life.

Further, stress is reduced in our lives when we can lay hold of a higher perspective about money. Firstly, stress is reduced when we keep the perspective that God is in our midst and that all we have belongs to God and is a gift from God. It makes a difference in the tension of dealing with money to know and to believe that my needs will be met by God who cares for me. Secondly, stress is reduced when we keep the perspective that my worth is not conditioned by the amount of money that I have or the value of belongings that I own.

This higher perspective on money is maintained when we consistently give away a portion of our income to others, even when our budgets are tight. Such giving is a protest against a consumer society that says I am only as good as what I own. Such giving is also a courageous act of faith that says God is the author and sustainer of my life even at the financial level.

Managing time

It was Shakespeare who wrote, "Short time seems long in sorrow's sharp sustaining." These words remind us of the flexibility of time. Each of us has the same amount of time each day and the actual measurement of time does not vary. However, how we fill our time makes time seem to expand or contract. In the moment of grief or boredom, time can drag. In the moment of excitement or pressure, time can race. We have some control over the pace of time, then, by how we fill our time and how we think about time.

Stress does result for some people because time drags and days never seem to end. Often this is the case in a state of temporary grief, or when we find ourselves in a place where we do not belong.

However, for most people in our culture the stress that results from time is due to a lack of time. Our cultural messages tell us that everything has to be fast: food is fast, copiers are fast, computers are fast, cars are fast, service is fast. Yet the faster these go, the less time we seem to have. We attempt to do one more thing—fast. Life is short, so let's squeeze in one more thing. Don't waste time because time is money. We live in an age that suffers from hurry sickness and incessant busyness. Thomas Merton said that such busyness is the most rampant form of violence today.

Ironically, as we ingest all the cultural messages about speed, time itself seems to contract. Long time seems short in hurry's harshness.

We can deal with the stress that comes from the pressure of time in at least two ways. Firstly, we can choose to fill our time with what is important to us. As with our money, our time needs to follow our life purposes. Time that flows like a river in a clear-cut channel directed by our life purposes brings us peace.

As with money we have to start by being clear about what we want to achieve in life. We might break it down to what we want to achieve this year. Then ask how my schedule this week gives priority to my life goals and how my schedule today gives priority to those goals. In our lives some things will not get done. In the lives of those who are stressed, what is not getting done are often the things that really are important life goals. In the lives of those who are less stressed, what does not get done are the things that are really not very important.

As we begin to look at what is and what is not getting done in our lives, it is often helpful at first to take a few days to write down exactly how we spend our time each day. With the facts staring us in the face we can make a conscious decision to shift our priorities. As well, we can choose not to overcommit by delegating some of the tasks that really belong to others and by learning to say "no" to requests for our time that really do not fit in with our life purpose.

Firstly, then, stress is lessened in our lives when we give purpose to our time. Time is less likely to contract on us when we are clear about what we want to do with our time. Secondly, time is less likely to contract on us and pressure us when we gain a different perspective about time. The shift has been described by one person as a shift from life being time-centered to that of time being life-centered. Rather than trying to cram life activities into a short amount of time, we can shift to think how this moment of time can be meaningful and fulfilling.

I can remember in my early days of parenting trying to set aside an hour each morning for prayer. No matter how early I got up for this quiet hour it seemed that at least one of my young children would get up shortly after I started and interrupt "my time." It seems ridiculous in retrospect, but this would make me angry. They had messed up my time. How would I ever deal with them, then have some time to myself and still do all that needed to be done in that day? I came to see that having a child in my lap was in itself my meditation. This moment was precious and not to be missed. When I let go of worry about time slipping away and focused on the meaning of the moment, time seemed to expand and stress was lessened.

This distinction between life as time-centered and time as life-centered is made in the two concepts of time expressed in the New Testament words *chronos* and *kairos*. *Chronos* is a word for intervals of time or the duration of time. When Jesus says in John 7:33, "I shall be with you a little longer, and then I go to him who sent me," he is talking about the duration of time. When, however, Paul says in Romans 5:6, "While we were yet helpless, at the right time Christ died for the ungodly," he is talking about *kairos* time. Stress is lessened in our lives when we shift from a preoccupation with *chronos* time and begin to participate in *kairos* time. In *kairos* time we participate in events of meaning instead of events of busyness. In *kairos* time we become sensitive to the right moment for action, or see the wonder of events that are perfectly timed in our lives. In *kairos* time, time itself seems to expand and the pressure of time is lifted.

Finally, in *kairos* time we learn to "waste time" for God. To set aside a day or a portion of a day as the Sabbath is in the eyes of the world wasting time. To set aside time for prayer or to sit and do nothing except enjoy the beauty around us is in the eyes of the world wasting time. Yet this time breaks the clutch of *chronos* time on our lives and the pressure is released.

I remember talking with an orthodox Jewish friend who was describing the observance of the Sabbath. My reaction was to say how restricting the Sabbath laws seemed to be. It seemed as if he could do very little on the Sabbath. His remark to me was, "This is not restricting at all. This is freedom. I am set free on the Sabbath from all the pressures of things to do that assault me all week long." "Wasting time" for God in fact brings us freedom, even freedom from stress.

Yet, to "waste time" for God will present us with a challenge—and this is perhaps why it is so hard for many of us to come out of the pressure of *chronos* time. In order to "waste time" for God we must grow comfortable with silence—the silence from which many of us run. For in the silence we meet ourselves: the parts we like and the parts we don't like. In the silence we also meet God and must face what God wants for our lives, some of which we will like and some of which we definitely will not like. In the silence our inner purpose and direction will emerge, which we can follow only by acts of faith. Then our lives will have a purpose and will follow a course like a river which has a clear-cut channel, a river that seems to have its beginning in something far higher than we are and that flows on beyond us into something eternal.

The Psalmist knew this when he wrote Psalm 46. The ability to remain without stress, even when the earth changes and the mountains shake, comes from an awareness of that river which flows from the holy habitation of the Most High. And the awareness of the river comes from the experience described in Psalm 46:10, "Be still and know that I am God."

Chapter Four
Stress and Our Relationships

"*Behold, how good and pleasant it is when brothers dwell in unity! It is like the dew of Hermon, which falls on the mountains of Zion. For there the Lord has commanded the blessing, life forevermore*" (Psalm 133:1-3).

In the scorching heat of the Judean desert, the dew created by the snow-capped Mount Hermon in the north was a refreshing and vital source of moisture each day. To use Hildegaard's phrase, it was indeed a "merciful dew." The stress of the heat for plants, animals, and people was mitigated by the dew of Hermon.

The Psalmist proclaims that our relationships can be like that dew, providing a source of blessing and real life. Without relationships we miss that merciful dew. But more than that, without a certain type of relationship where there is a deep unity, we miss that merciful dew.

Stress without relationships

Research has shown that relationships which provide social support are vital during times of stress. Scientist Eric Lindemann found in his research of survivors of the Cocoanut Grove fire in which 129 people were killed that those survivors who had plenty of human contact and emotional support recovered more quickly. Some of these even had greater levels of self-esteem and well-being after the stress-producing tragedy.

Other research has shown that people with quality social supports which come through marriage, close friendships, extended families, church memberships, or group associations have a far lower mortality rate than those who do not have such relationships. As well, in the research on burnout it has been documented that social supports at work and at home can serve as a buffer to the job stresses that lead to burnout.

Scripture also indicates that men and women were not made to be alone. The primeval history of Genesis declares of man in the Garden that it is not good to be alone (Genesis 2). Sin is described as creating a separation between men and women and God (Genesis 3), as well as creating separation between family members

(Genesis 4). The New Testament message proclaims that life lived abundantly is life lived in a relationship with Christ. In that relationship the separation with God is overcome, and we are taught how to love one another.

Whether scientific or scriptural, the evidence is clear: our social support networks found in families, friends, churches, and groups enable us to live longer and to confront the stresses of life more effectively. Our relationships are truly a "merciful dew."

Stress within relationships

Yet, relationships also can cause stress. Psychologists tell us that our deepest anxieties about life emerge in relationships that matter to us. Further, most of us know the tension that is created in our lives when we are at odds with someone who is close to us. The "merciful dew" of relationships comes when there is a "living together in unity," according to the Psalmist.

This "living together in unity" is not some merging together where people lose their personhood, for this would create more stress. Even in scripture (Genesis 2:24) where it speaks of a man leaving his father and mother and cleaving to his wife to become one flesh there is maintained a careful balance between independence and interdependence in the "oneness" or unity. The Hebrew word *davak*, which means to cleave or cling in this passage, is used elsewhere in scripture of the joining together of the scales on a crocodile's back (Job 41:9), of the scales on a breastplate of armor (1 Kings 22:34), and of the con-

nection of the wings of the cherubim (2 Chronicles 3:12). The image is of something connected for the good of the whole, yet able to operate with a certain independence. It is this kind of unity that is a stress reliever in relationships and provides for a "merciful dew."

In the language of our day we might speak of healthy relationships as those which keep *boundaries* without creating *barriers*. To set boundaries in a relationship is to say that we have the power as a person to say "no," or to take care of ourselves and to let others take care of themselves. Those who set healthy boundaries are saying in essence, "I will not be God to take care of your needs and I will not expect you to be God to take care of mine. Instead, I will find my strength from the kingdom of God within me (Luke 17:21), and with that strength I will choose to be in a relationship with you. I value you for being a 'merciful dew' in my life but you are not my 'living spring of water' that can never dry up."

The language used by those who keep healthy boundaries is the language of assertiveness. Assertiveness means to be clear, firm, and honest in our relationships without being aggressive or passive. Theologian Paul Tillich would say that assertiveness is where love and power are held in balance. Aggressiveness is loveless power—for example, you do something to upset me and I chew you out and call you names. Passiveness is powerless love—for example, you do something to upset me and I say it is all right and never tell you how I am hurt. When we are assertive we maintain our own sense of power but react with the balancing effect of love—for example, you do something to upset me and I tell you clearly how it made me feel and firmly what I need you to do about it.

When Jesus is called by Mary and Martha to come and heal Lazarus (John 11) he waits for two days before responding. During that time, Lazarus dies. When Jesus finally does come, he is met on the way first by Martha and then by Mary asking him why he did not come sooner and keep Lazarus from dying. The responses of Mary and Martha exemplify assertiveness. With tears and words they convey their emotion and upset saying directly, "Lord, if you had been here, my brother would not have died." Jesus' response is also an assertive one. Firstly, he came in his own time when he felt it was right. He was not too quick to show how nice he was or how he could please others. Secondly, he too could show emotion and also state clearly and firmly that, "Your brother will rise again." There was no shouting or belittling. There was no people-pleasing. There was no pretending as if nothing had happened. Here were people with healthy boundaries sharing their feelings in a stressful situation.

To set boundaries, however, does not mean that we create barriers. When we set boundaries we are aware that we can choose to let people in close to our deepest heart. Sometimes we choose to exclude people from closeness with us, but sometimes we choose to include people in a special closeness.

When we create barriers, we are not able to choose. Virtually everyone is excluded from closeness in order to protect us from exposure of an area of life that shows our weakness, or evokes feelings of shame and vulnerability. Even those who can help and nurture us at our point of weakness are excluded because the risk is too great. There is a constant source of stress in attempting to maintain the barriers. Also, there is a constant source of stress in worrying about what will happen if someone sees us as we really are.

When we make the shift from living with barriers to living with boundaries, we also make a shift in our language, choosing to include high levels of conversational intimacy in our speaking with important others. Rev. David Luecke points out that there are five levels of intimacy in our conversation: (1) the lowest level of intimacy is in the conversation about facts and information; (2) a low level of intimacy is in the conversation about the ideas of others; (3) a moderate level of intimacy is in the conversation about our own ideas and opinions; (4) a high level of intimacy is in the conversation that reveals personal information about ourselves; (5) the highest level of intimacy is in conversation that reveals our personal feelings about another person right now. When we choose to live without barriers, we become more comfortable using levels four and five in this schema of conversational intimacy.

Further, when we make the shift from living with barriers to living with boundaries, we discover the secret of those words given to the apostle Paul in his weakness, "My grace is sufficient for you, for my power is made perfect in weakness" (2 Corinthians 12:9). It is at our point of weakness—when we feel most vulnerable or ashamed—that we are closest to the power for living. When we hide and deny our weaknesses, we miss the power and increase stress in our lives. When we choose to risk revealing the weaker and less acceptable side of ourselves, we find the power.

To live with one other person, or to live in community with other persons, where we are accepted with our weaknesses and held accountable for our weaknesses, may initially bring with it a level of stress. Yet, in the long term the move from barriers to boundaries where independence and interdependence are kept in balance makes for a "living together in unity" and a "merciful dew" that saves us from the "heat of the day."

Chapter Five
Stress and Our Thinking

"And a great storm arose, and the waves beat into the boat, so that the boat was already filling.... And he awoke and rebuked the wind, and said to the sea, 'Peace! Be still!'.... He said to them, 'Why are you afraid? Have you no faith'" (Mark 4:37-40)?

How we think about an event has a lot to do with our emotional reaction to an event. Given the same experience of the wind and waves that the disciples were having, Jesus was not experiencing stress at all. In fact, he was having a good nap in the boat. But the disciples' reaction to the same event was one of intense stress. They thought that they were going to perish and they thought that Jesus did not care. This thinking led to fear.

The importance of thinking in our assessment of life events has a long history. Two thousand years ago Epictetus wrote, "Men are disturbed not by things but by the views which they take of things." Shakespeare wrote, "There is nothing good or bad, but thinking makes it so." Even prior to these it was written in Proverbs 23:7, "As a man thinketh in his heart, so is he." In his research on stress Hans Selye came to the conclusion that it is not so much what happens to us that makes a difference, but the way we take it. Other researchers have found that there is an intricate process of appraisal that happens for each of us in response to any life event: an appraisal of the meaning of the event itself and an appraisal of our ability to cope with the event.

Distortions in our appraisal of meaning

A number of writers, such as Albert Ellis, Aaron T. Beck and David Burns, have pointed out that much of our negative emotion in life comes from our thinking that is distorted. If we stop and listen to our thinking, we will often find patterns to our thinking that distort reality and skew it in a negative direction. This negativity creates stress in our lives.

Often we distort the meaning of an event in the following ways:

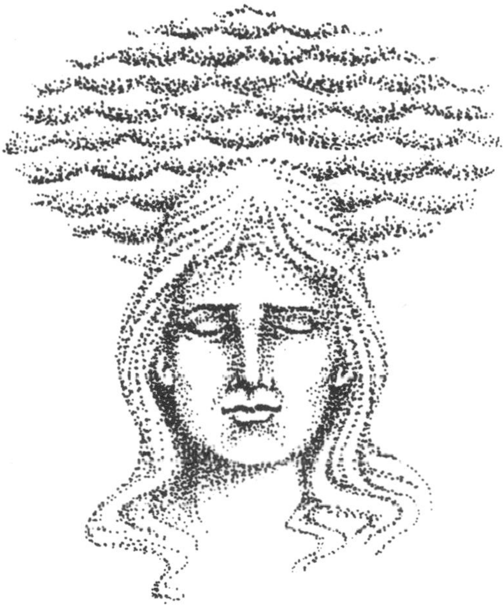

1. We make a catastrophe out of an event. This is the classic "mountain out of a mole hill" thinking. In the story of the wind and the waves the disciples thought they were going to die. This distortion led to intense stress. In reality they were experiencing a storm that would pass.

2. We overgeneralize, taking an event out of context and seeing it as a pattern of continual defeat. Scripture does not tell us, but perhaps there was one disciple who was thinking, "This is just like my luck to end up in a boat in the middle of a storm. There is always a cloud over my head anyway and this just proves it." Such thinking would not have been realistic or helpful.

3. We jump to conclusions. The disciples jumped to the conclusion that Jesus did not care and was not going to help in this situation. They evidently thought that they could read his mind and predict what was going to happen. They were wrong in their thinking, and it only increased their level of stress.

4. We see events in all or nothing categories. Perhaps one of the disciples was thinking that because Jesus has not gotten up in the last ten minutes he is never going to get up. Or, if Jesus really loved us he would never have allowed something like this to happen. People who love you do not do these kinds of things. Such thinking has little flexibility and produces stress.

5. We filter out the positive aspects in an event. In order to end up being afraid, the disciples had to filter out the reality of Jesus being with them and the remembrance of his power. A less stressful thought would have

been to think how good it was that Jesus came along and that in the midst of disaster he had always proved to be helpful and powerful.

These are just a few of the distortions of meaning that can come in response to life events. Each of us has our own unique set of distortions that we can begin to identify if we will stop to listen when the winds and the waves beset us.

Distortions in our ability to cope

How we think of our own abilities and resources often gets distorted as well. Some examples of these distortions are as follows:

1. We belittle our abilities and identify with our mistakes. Instead of saying that they misjudged the weather on the sea that day, the disciples might have said that they were no good as sailors and would never be able to get out of this mess. Further, they might have said that they were fools for following Jesus. Look where it got them. This distorted thinking would have robbed them of the ability to guide the ship through the storm.

2. We blame ourselves when it is not our fault. One of the disciples might have been thinking that if only he had not suggested the boat ride this would never have happened. Or, if he had not been short-tempered with Jesus earlier in the day maybe Jesus would care more.

This type of thinking robs us of the ability to ask, "What can I do now to alleviate the problem?"

3. We forget about our past successes and what actions we took before. I wonder how often the disciples had sailed on that same sea and encountered the same kind of storm and managed to get through it. What did they do then?

4. We forget about others around us with whom we could band together for help. Instead of thinking that they were isolated, the disciples could have thought of what they could do together to get the boat through the storm. Their combined talents probably would have been sufficient even without disturbing Jesus from his nap.

5. We wear an ethical straight-jacket that keeps us from using all of our resources. These are often easily identified because they include the words "should" or "shouldn't." Perhaps one of the disciples thought that he shouldn't bother Jesus even though Jesus was a great resource in this situation. Maybe a disciple thought that he shouldn't get upset or show his anger in this situation. Maybe he shouldn't tell God how he feels. Maybe it was the Sabbath, and they were restricted as to how they could respond.

6. We make up our own Sabbath rules and spiritual commandments that operate more powerfully than the actual Biblical commandments. Sometimes we have taken over these powerful traditions from our own families. These internal commandments often restrict our

ability to cope in stressful situations. Even worse, some of these actually create the stress in the first place.

Perhaps one of the disciples lived with an internal commandment such as, "Thou shalt always be the perfect disciple." This would have only isolated him from the other disciples and restricted his ability to get help. The result would have been increased stress.

Modern day disciples live with many unscriptural commandments like: (a) "Thou shalt never talk about your problems"; (b) "Thou shalt make lots of money"; (c) "Thou shalt never play until all the work is done"; (d) "Thou shalt never think highly of thyself"; (e) "Thou shalt love everyone else but not thyself." These commandments lead to distorted thinking and restrict our ability to respond with all our resources in a stressful situation. Again, these commandments and distortions are unique for each of us and need to be identified by us when the winds and the waves beset us.

Thinking realistically

If our thinking is distorted we must find a way to think more realistically. This is not always easy because many of our thoughts are automatic, meaning that they come quickly and we are not always aware of them.

The trick is, firstly, to begin to *notice events* that produce stress in our lives and, when they occur, to stop and listen to our thinking. Secondly, we must *write down* what is going through our heads in order to identify our thoughts. Thirdly, we can *rate how strong* our emotion is. (For example, how anxious are we on a scale of 1–10.) Fourthly, we can *ask ourselves how realistic* is the thought and give it a percentage rating. (For example, the disciples might have said, "Now that I think about it we have some resources and the likelihood of our perishing is probably only about 25%.") Fifthly, we can *rerate our emotion* to see how much it has lessened as the result of our realistic assessment. (For example, after thinking more realistically the disciples might have noticed that their anxiety had dropped to a level of a 1 or a 2.) Sixthly, we can go on to *assess the consequences* of our distorted thinking even if it does come true. (For example, a disciple might have thought, "Even if the boat capsizes does that mean we will all perish? Are there not other things that we can do to get to shore?")

Thinking more realistically about a situation helps to ease our emotions and lower our perception of an event as stressful. When the winds and waves beset us, it is a good time to stop and begin writing.

Thinking hopefully

Realistic thinking and hopeful thinking are both different from the more popular positive thinking. Positive thinking at its worst asks us to look through the world with rose-colored glasses and believe that everything is all right. At its best it is an attempt to envision the best possible outcome and keep one's mind focused on it. The problem with positive thinking is that it is hard to sustain. Distorted and negative thinking creep back in.

Realistic thinking takes a rational and objective approach. It helps us isolate our distorted thoughts and rationally reassess them. It uses the power of our rational human minds to do this.

Hopeful thinking holds on to the belief that no matter how difficult the situation might be, God will be with us in it. Maybe God is calling us to a new level of faith in this difficulty. Maybe God is enabling us to learn and grow in this difficulty. Maybe God is just with us, and that is enough.

Unlike positive thinking, hopeful thinking sees the danger, the pain, and the tension realistically. There are no rose-colored glasses with hopeful thinking. Hopeful thinking can stare evil in the face and still be hopeful.

Unlike realistic thinking, hopeful thinking does not limit our coping ability to human rationality. It goes beyond human ability and rationality to acknowledge that we are not alone in this life-journey unless we choose to be. God is with us. Even more, hopeful thinking carries with it a presupposition about this life-journey: namely, that even when it is hard for us to see it, all things are working for our good.

Finally, hopeful thinking says that what we perceive as a disaster may be God attempting to draw near to us in a new way. Every time God or the angels approach humans in scripture they first have to say, "Be not afraid!" Our normal human reaction to the coming of God is fear or upset. Could it be that in the upsetting events of life, God is merely attempting to draw near to us? The disciples in the boat thought that they were about to perish. In fact, God was merely trying to draw close and show them who Christ really was.

Could it be that when we perceive the threatening winds and waves of life God is merely attempting to bring a little "water" into our lives? But because we have been so "dry" for so long we perceive the "water" as a threatening storm.

Chapter Six
Stress and Our Illusions

"When Jesus saw him and knew that he had been lying there a long time, he said to him, 'Do you want to be healed?' The sick man answered him, 'Sir I have no man to put me into the pool when the water is troubled, and while I am going another steps down before me'" (John 5:6-7).

Living with illusions

We all live with illusions. For much of life we live with the illusion that we will not die, or our loved ones will not die. Every time we get into a car and race down the highway at sixty miles per hour, we live with an illusion that we are safe and that we will not be hurt in a crash. Many of us live with an illusion of control: that if we live correctly, somehow the unpredictability of natural events, sickness or disease will not affect us.

We also live with illusions about other people and how the events of life will turn out for us. The man whom Jesus found lying beside the pool of Bethzatha had been there for thirty-eight years. He had learned to live with the illusion that no one would help him and that life would repeat itself. Every time the waters would be stirred up, someone else would get into the waters first, and he would not have a chance to be healed. His illusion was so strong that he had given up on any hope of being healed. So Jesus asks him if he even wants to be healed.

Repeated events in our own lives lead us to develop our own unique illusions. Living with an alcoholic parent can lead to the illusion that other people are not to be trusted and that one's own thoughts and feelings are not to be shared or valued. Having been raised in poverty, we might live with an illusion that poverty is all we deserve, or we might reverse the illusion and feel that we are nothing unless we have a certain amount of money in the bank. If at one point in our lives we experienced a number of traumatic or chaotic events, we might now live with the illusion that life is out to get us or that bad luck will follow us all the days of our lives.

We can live with cultural illusions. During World War II any news reports coming out of Japan that would help us to see the Japanese people in a favorable light were suppressed because we were living with the illusion that all Japanese were evil. The same thing was true about the Russians during periods of the Cold War. These illusions were often accompanied by illusions of our own country being righteous and without malice. I remember making a pilgrimage to the religious community of Taizé in southern France and entering into group discussions with young persons from around the world. I had lived for a long time with the illusion that our country was the most honorable and helpful country in the world. But my illusion was challenged when I listened to fellow Christians from Africa talk about economic policies that robbed them of their resources and left them in worse poverty than before, under the guise of helping them to be better off.

Often we live with illusions about our personal goodness or righteousness. In a marriage we might live with the illusion that it is all the other person's fault that the marriage is in trouble. In a society we might live with the illusion that "those other people" are leading to the decay of life. In a religious community we might live with the illusion that it is that "other group" who is wrong and who will experience the judgment of God. Jesus reserved his harshest words for people operating with such illusions saying, "Woe to you, scribes and Pharisees, hypocrites! for you are like whitewashed tombs, which outwardly appear beautiful, but within they are full of dead men's bones and all uncleanness" (Matthew 23:27).

We all live with illusions.

It is true that sometimes our illusions help to eliminate stress in our lives. For us to be able to function on a day to day basis we need illusions of safety and life. We would not be able to function because of the overwhelming stress if we thought we could die every time we got into the car or if each day we feared the death of a loved one.

Illusions of childhood help us to survive childhood. To live with continued childlike trust and an open innocence in a family where we are manipulated and our feelings are thrown back in our face to hurt us would mean our psychological destruction. To survive, we have to develop the illusion that no one can be trusted and we must always be on the defense. Our illusions help us to survive and to lessen the stress of life.

Yet there are at least three ways in which our illusions are associated with stress in our lives. Firstly, there are times when our illusions are shattered by the events of life. Someone we love dies. Someone runs a stop sign and crashes into our car. A hurricane or flood destroys all that we own. Stress invades our lives as we attempt to piece back together our illusions about safety and control.

Secondly, sometimes our illusions that eliminated stress at one point in our lives now actually create stress. When the child who operated with the illusion that no one in life could be trusted grows up and gets married, severe stress can occur when the partner wants emotional intimacy. The person who put all of his or her hope and security in a charismatic authority figure may experience severe stress when the authority figure suddenly changes the rules or asks the person to do something that violates their conscience.

Thirdly, the path to emotional and spiritual maturity (whether we choose the path or the path is chosen for us) leads us to points where we are challenged to change the way we "see." The Psalmist challenged the illusions of worldly power and prestige when he wrote, "Men of low estate are but a breath, men of high estate are a delusion" (Psalm 62:9). Jesus repeatedly said to his listeners, "He who has eyes to see, let him see." Or to a man who had just received his physical and spiritual sight Jesus said, "For judgment I came into this world, that those who do not see may see, and that those who see may become blind" (John 9:39). In order to grow, our illusions about ourselves and our world must change.

Such changes create stress. This is why we work so hard to resist changing the way we see. W. H. Auden wrote, "We would rather be ruined than changed, we would rather die in our dread than climb the cross of the moment and let our illusions die." This also led Thomas Merton to wonder if there were twenty men or women in the whole world who might see things as they really are. He concluded that there were probably only one or two such persons in the whole world but that they were the ones who were really holding the world together.

While our illusions may at times be helpful, intense stress can occur when our illusions are shattered or called to change. Such times are like the "stirring of the waters" in the pool of Bethzatha that called the paralytic to look at his illusions.

Learning to "see"

By learning to "see" we can lessen the intensity of the stress created by our illusions. We do not have to await a time of intense stress before we start to work on our illusions. We can do preventive or preparatory work in the following ways:

1. Developing a daily life of prayer. A life of prayer and the simple reading of scripture on a daily basis works to shatter our illusions about life. We need only take fifteen minutes a day to read a few verses of scripture and then in prayer reflect on their meaning for our lives.

The Psalmist suffered from the illusion that life was biased against him and in favor of the rich. Then he went into the sanctuary and perceived things entirely differently (Psalm 73:17). Likewise, when we enter into our own sanctuary with God, we begin to see life differently. Confronted daily with the paradoxes of scripture in which we are challenged to love the enemy, to reflect on our darkness in order to find light, to discover strength through weakness, to find happiness in association with the poor rather than with the rich, our illusions are eroded little by little. It is as if through a life of prayer and reading of scripture Jesus asks us if we want to be healed of our illusions that are limiting us—illusions that we have held onto for a long time like the man beside the pool of Bethzatha.

2. Developing familiarity with the symbolic. The deeper meanings about life often can be conveyed only through symbols. This is why Jesus spoke in parables and the prophets wrote in poetry. When our illusions are being challenged, a new way of seeing will often be presented to us through the symbolism contained in scripture, poetry, music or dreams. If we do not have the capacity for listening to the symbolic, our ability to see our present illusion and to glimpse a new level of meaning is frustrated and our stress is increased. In a time in which I suffered from the illusion that I was somebody special because of my academic success in seminary, I had a dream in which I threw a bust of my Old Testament professor out of a plane and it landed in a cemetery. I got the message that I needed this old way of living to die, because it was killing me.

The reading of good literature, listening to quality music, journaling of our thoughts and feelings, and the recording of our dreams all begin to acquaint us with the symbolic. Getting a notebook and keeping it beside our bed to record our dreams upon waking is a good way to start this process.

3. Developing a repentant attitude. In scripture the one who prepares the way of the Lord is John the Baptist. His message is the message of repentance. Jesus always follows this one. Likewise, the coming of the Lord

to give us new vision often follows a time when we are repentant and are open to seeing.

Having a repentant attitude does not mean feeling guilty or feeling awful about ourselves. It is an attitude that says we are open to turning our lives around; we are open to new sight. It can be as simple as finding ourselves in a conflict and stopping to ask, "What is my part in this conflict? How can I react differently?" It can be as profound as saying, "The way I have done my life has led to this mess. Help me find a new way to live."

4. Seeing from the point of view of eternity. We can begin each day asking for Christ to be present with us in the events of that day. This evokes the perspective of eternity in all that we do. To be able to see Christ present in frustrating events and frustrating people challenges our illusions about these encounters and lessens our stress.

But, further, we can stop and ask at the problematic times in life how this event might be different if I were in heaven looking back at it. Even to place ourselves a week or a year into the future will sometimes give us an entirely different perspective on a stressful event. We can imagine what we have learned and how things worked out.

The perspective of eternity adds even more because it challenges our driving assumptions about life. For instance, for the one suffering from the illusion of materialism to hear that there are no luggage racks on hearses begins to add the perspective of eternity and to challenge the illusion. For the one suffering from the illusion of

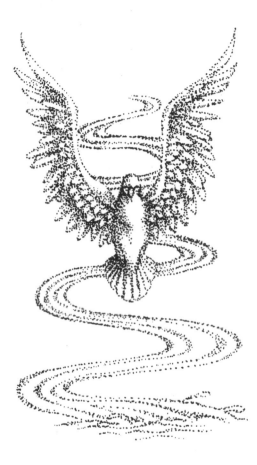

workaholism to hear that when one gets to heaven no one will ever ask you why you did not spend more time in the office begins to add the perspective of eternity and to challenge the illusion.

However, in learning to "see," not all of our work can be preventive or preparatory. Sometimes the events of life shatter our illusions, and we struggle to make meaning out of our existence. These times call for us to fall back upon our most basic beliefs and images about life. Not every belief or image is capable of sustaining us in these times. However, the basic beliefs and images distilled in the core sacraments of the church can often help us make the transition from our shattered illusions to new meaning in life. Two examples are those of Baptism and the Eucharist:

1. Baptism reminds us that even in the stressful and apparently meaningless times of life, we are children of God and we belong to One who will not leave us or forsake us and is constantly working for our good. Baptism also reminds us of the pattern of growth—namely, that of cross, death, burial, and resurrection. When our illusions are shattered, it is likely that our transition to new meaning will follow the same pattern of our baptism that is itself a symbol of the journey of Christ. We, too, will experience these events of life like a cross. We, too, will feel that we will die and that we are being buried. We, too, will experience new life through this and feel that we have

had a resurrection. The assurance of this pattern gives us meaning when our illusions are shattered.

2. The Eucharist reminds us that Christ is mysteriously present in the brokenness of our lives. Even though we cannot see it or rationally explain it, Christ is working with us and for us. Further, the Eucharist reminds us that we will be fed; we will have the physical, emotional, and spiritual sustenance to make it through this time of transition and God will supply our need.

Life is often like waiting beside the pool of Bethzatha; we are waiting for the next time the waters of life get stirred up. And when the waters are stirred up we experience stress, not the least of which is because our illusions about life are called to the surface. Jesus asks us in these times if we want to be healed and then proceeds to break our illusions about how life can be.

Chapter Seven
Conclusion

"On the last day of the feast, the great day, Jesus stood up and proclaimed, 'If anyone thirst, let him come to me and drink. He who believes in me as the scripture has said, "Out of his heart shall flow rivers of living water" '" *(John 7:37-38).*

It was a wise woman who posed the question to me and gave me the insight when she said, "Do you know why the Dead Sea is dead? It is because there is a stream that flows into it, but there is no stream that flows out of it. It receives, but it does not give."

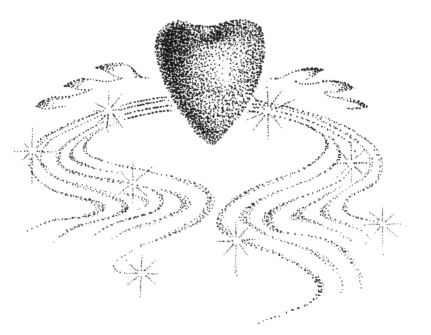

Working on stress in our lives is something like that. We can take in all the insights and remedial suggestions about stress, but it is all dead if we do nothing with it. This book has suggested ideas to contemplate and actions to take in dealing with stress. Using both contemplation and action will set up a flow—a flowing in and a flowing out—that will alleviate the worst effects of stress.

It is not important to do everything at once. We can start small. What is the simplest notion onto which we can hold? What is the smallest step that we can take? To make any change in our lives will start the flow.

Once we make a start, then we can make a plan. What is the next image onto which we can hold? What is the next easiest action for us to take? Then map out in steps of increasing difficulty those actions that need to be taken to lessen life's stress. For example, maybe the easiest step for me is to get a journal this week for the purpose of recording my thoughts, feelings, and dreams. The next step for me is to begin recording. The next step is to start with one day of exercise. The next step is to begin a prayer time. Perhaps the hardest step for me is to begin to speak intimately with someone. But I make a plan and begin to move along in that plan in the order of increasing difficulty.

The other approach to keep in mind is to seek balance in all the areas of our lives. Ideally we would find something to contemplate and act upon in all the areas that confront us with stress: our bodies, our environment, our relationships, our thinking, and our illusions.

However, some areas of our lives may be more difficult to change than others. In the short run, for example, it may not be possible to change much about our environment. Then we need to balance out the total level of stress in our lives by making extra efforts in other areas, like our relationships or our bodies.

A spiritual approach to stress acknowledges that there are available to us the resources for dealing with stress in life. Some of these resources are within us. Some come from beyond us. But there is no need to go through life as if we were desperately "thirsty" and about to "dry up." We are able to receive. We are responsible for what we do with the gift. We live at our best when there is a flow like a river.

Other Books in the Series

Little Pieces of Light...Darkness and Personal Growth
    by Joyce Rupp

Lessons from the Monastery That Touch Your Life
    by M. Basil Pennington, O.C.S.O.

As You and the Abused Person Journey Together
    by Sharon E. Cheston